Design Your Own Cars

Copyright © 2020 by SketchPert Press

All rights reserved. This book or any portion thereof

may not be reproduced or used in any manner whatsoever

without the express written permission of the publisher

except for the use of brief quotations in a book review.

Printed in the United States of America

9798697548950

INSTRUCTIONS

In the following pages you will find several blank templates. Use them to add your own unique elements such a stars, lightning bolts, emojis, or anything else you can think of. Be creative!

BEFORE

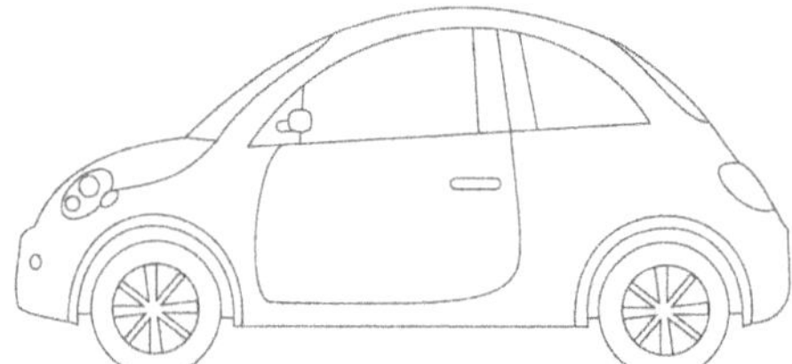

AFTER

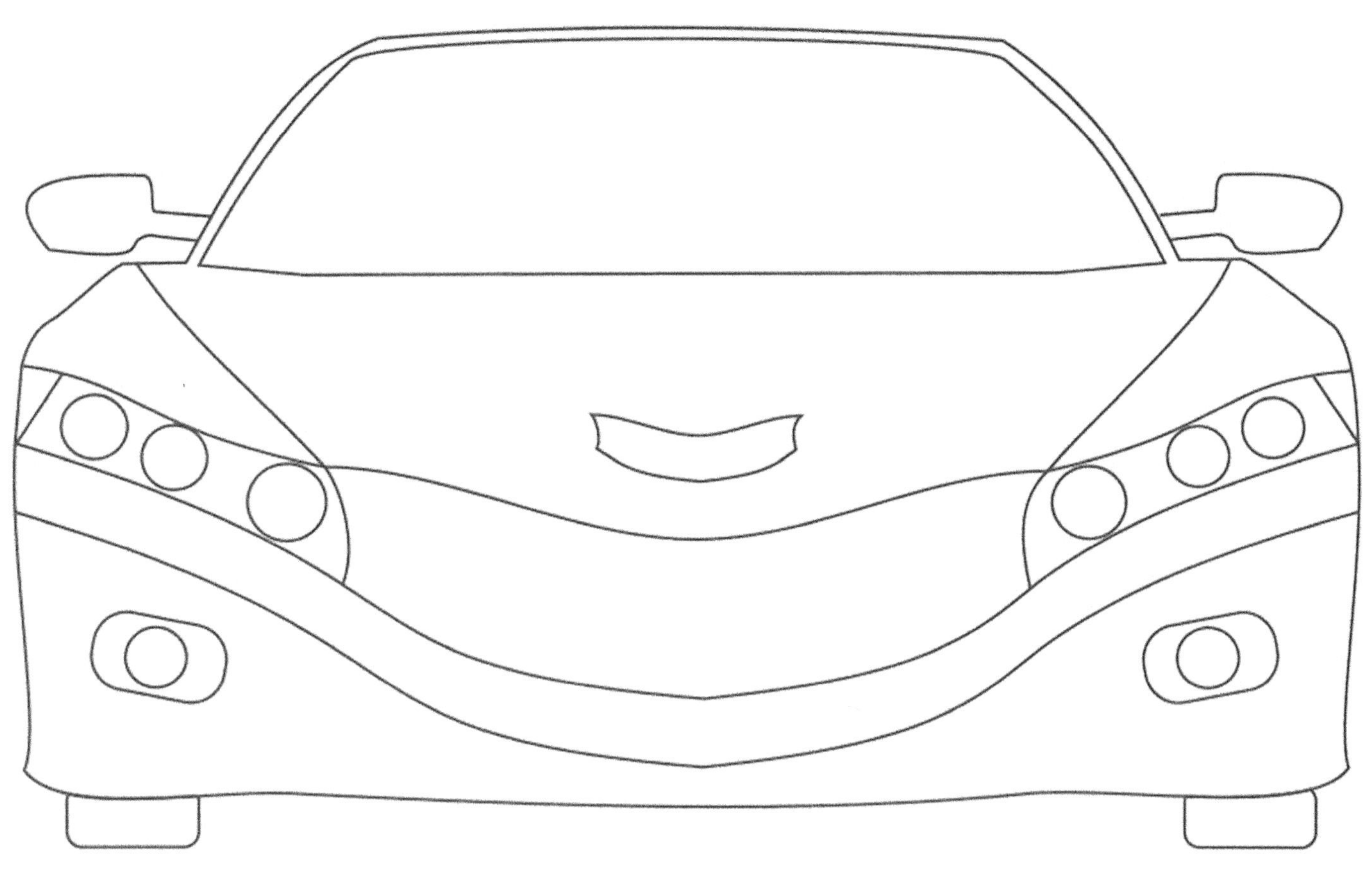

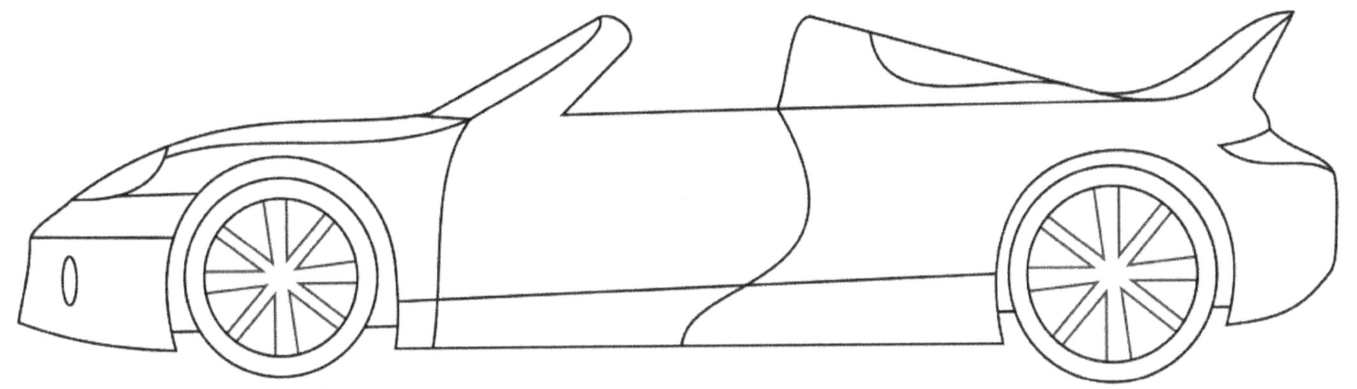

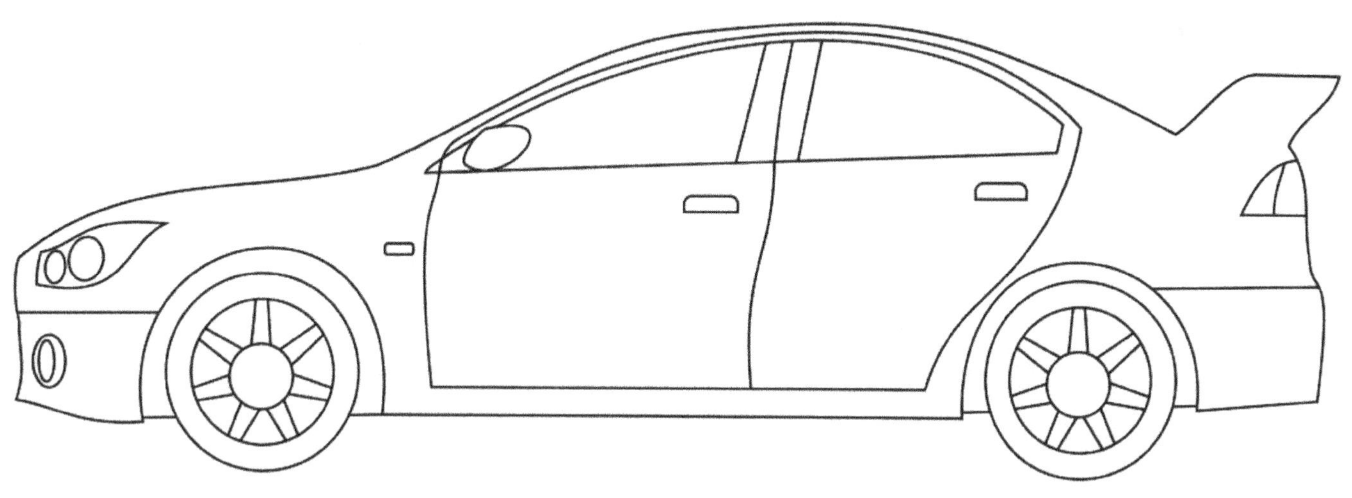

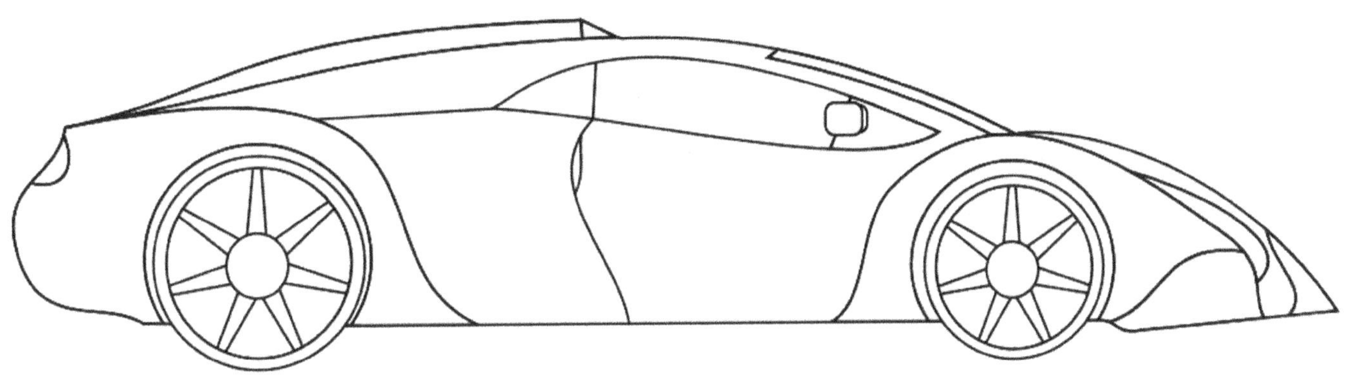

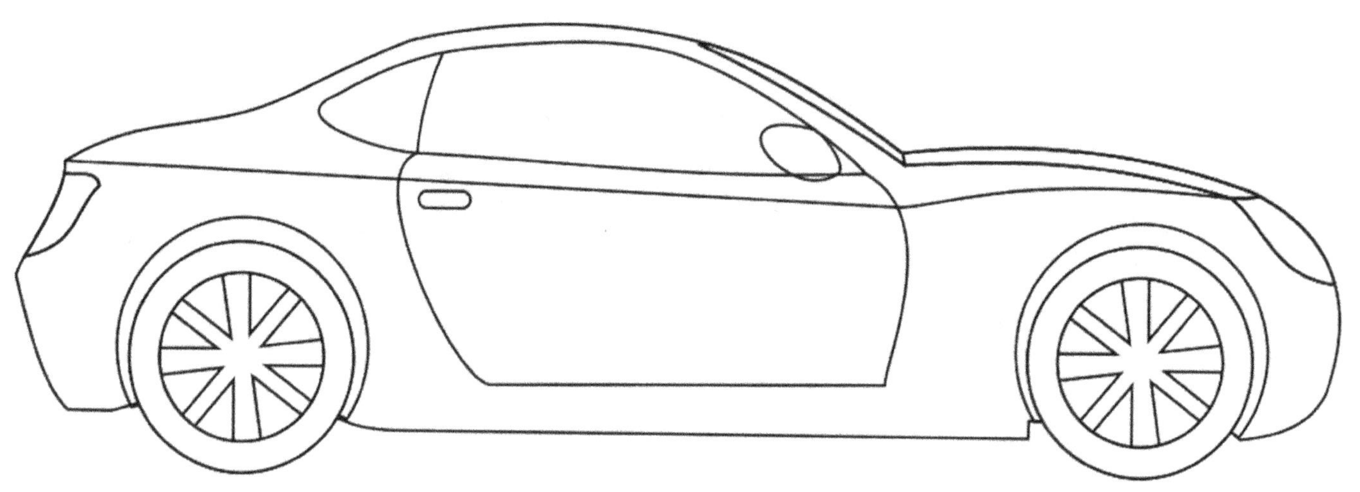

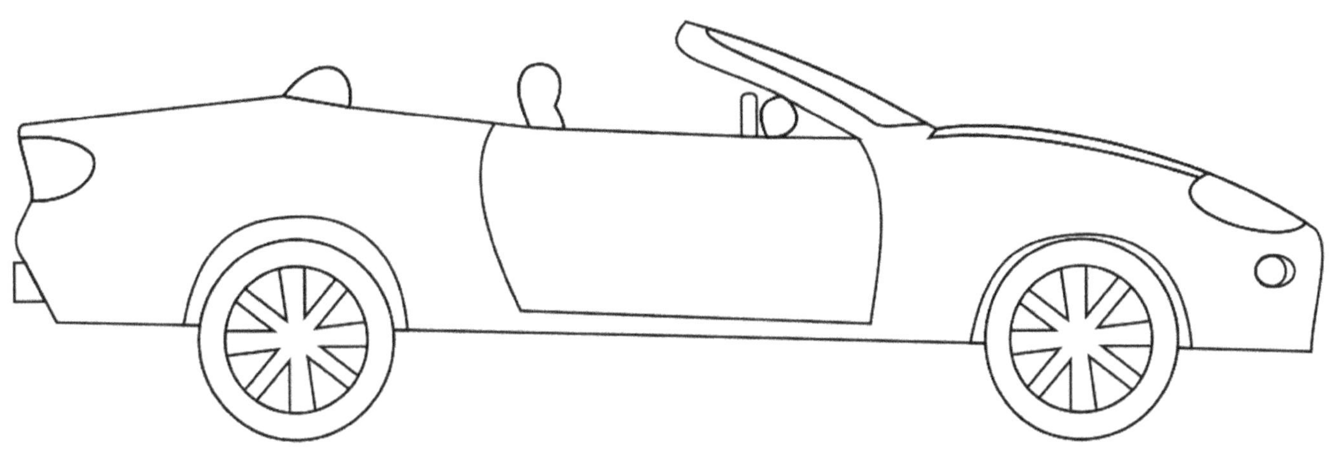

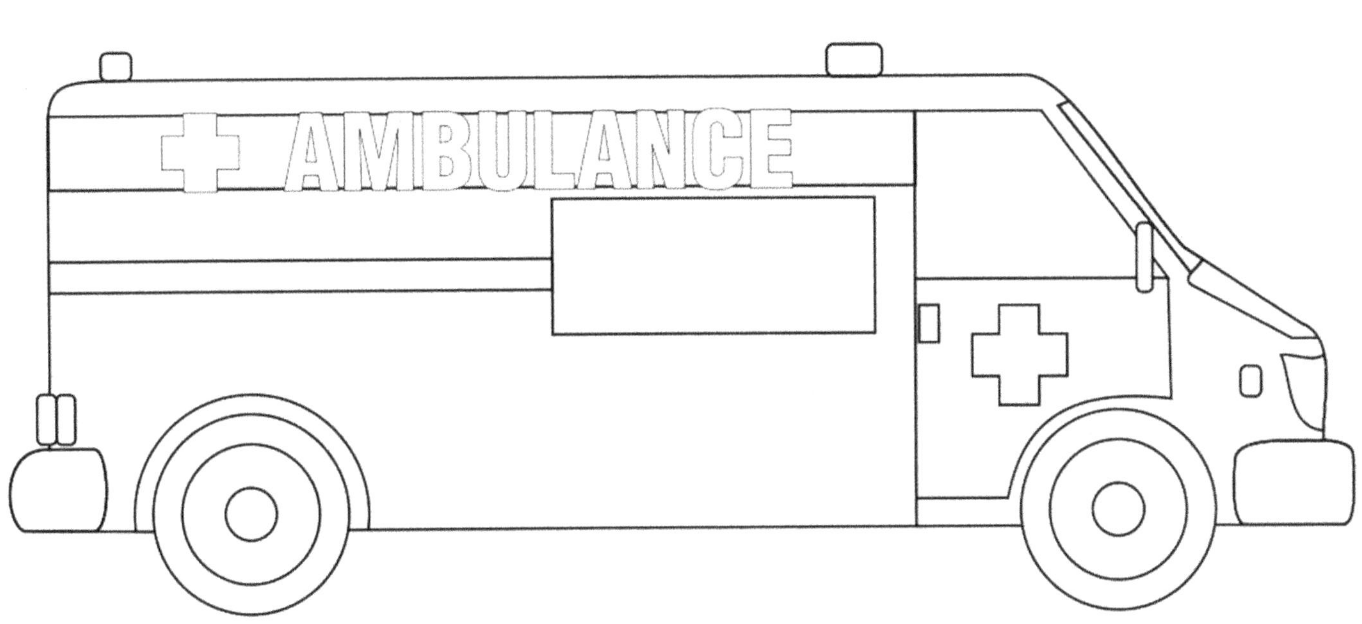

AMBULANCE

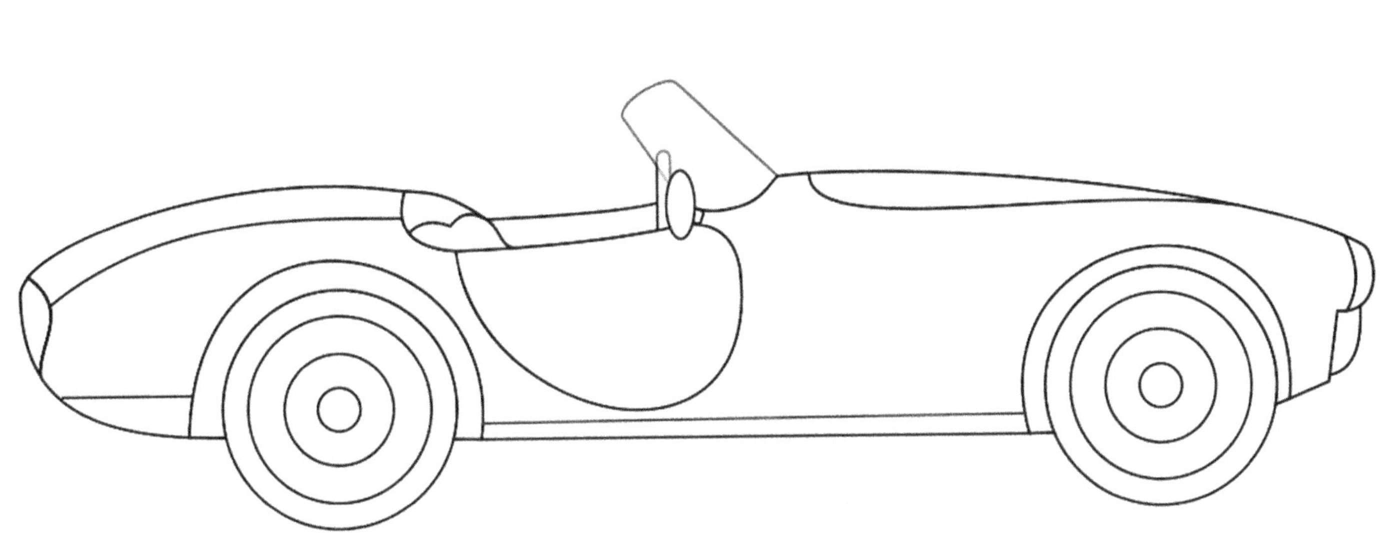

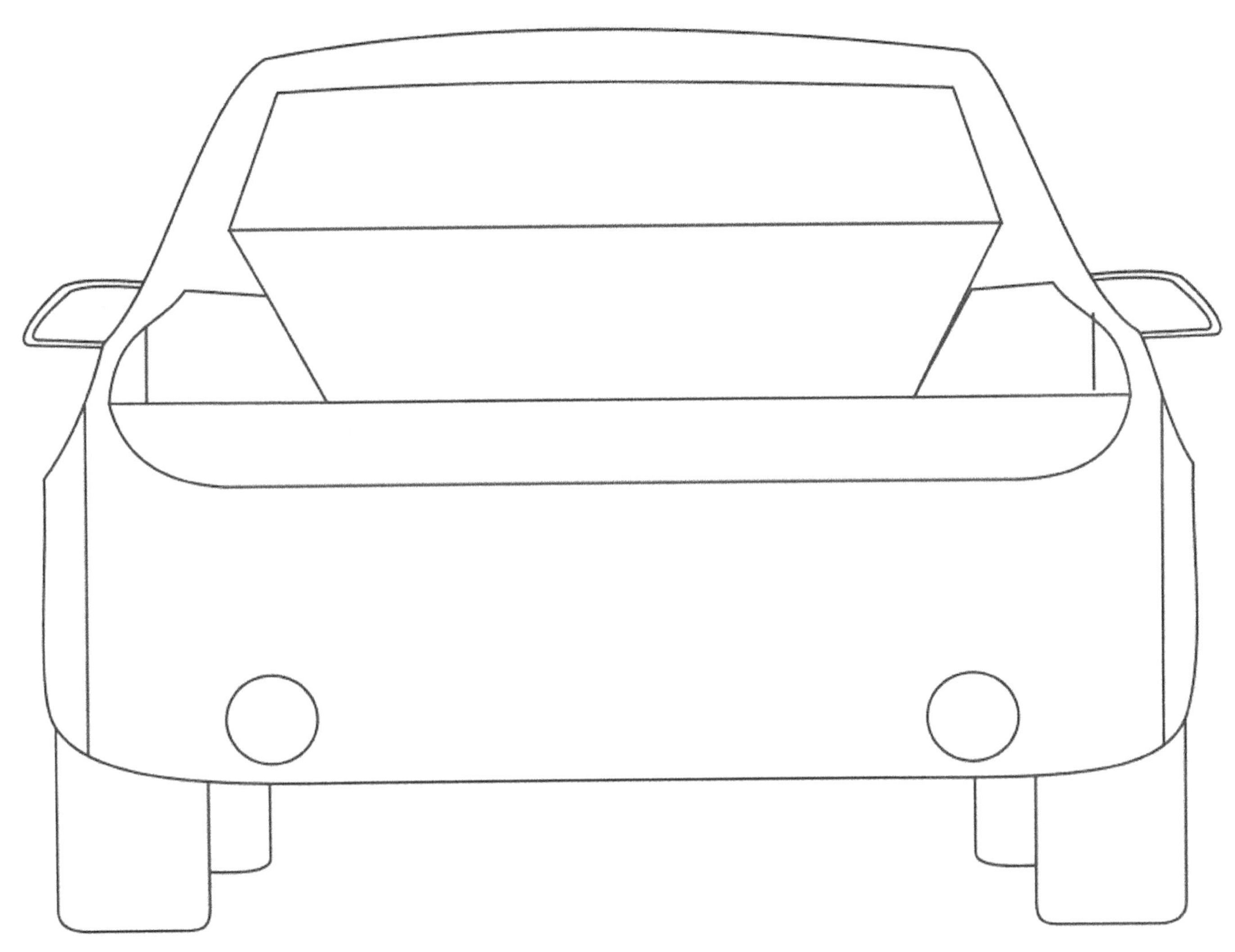

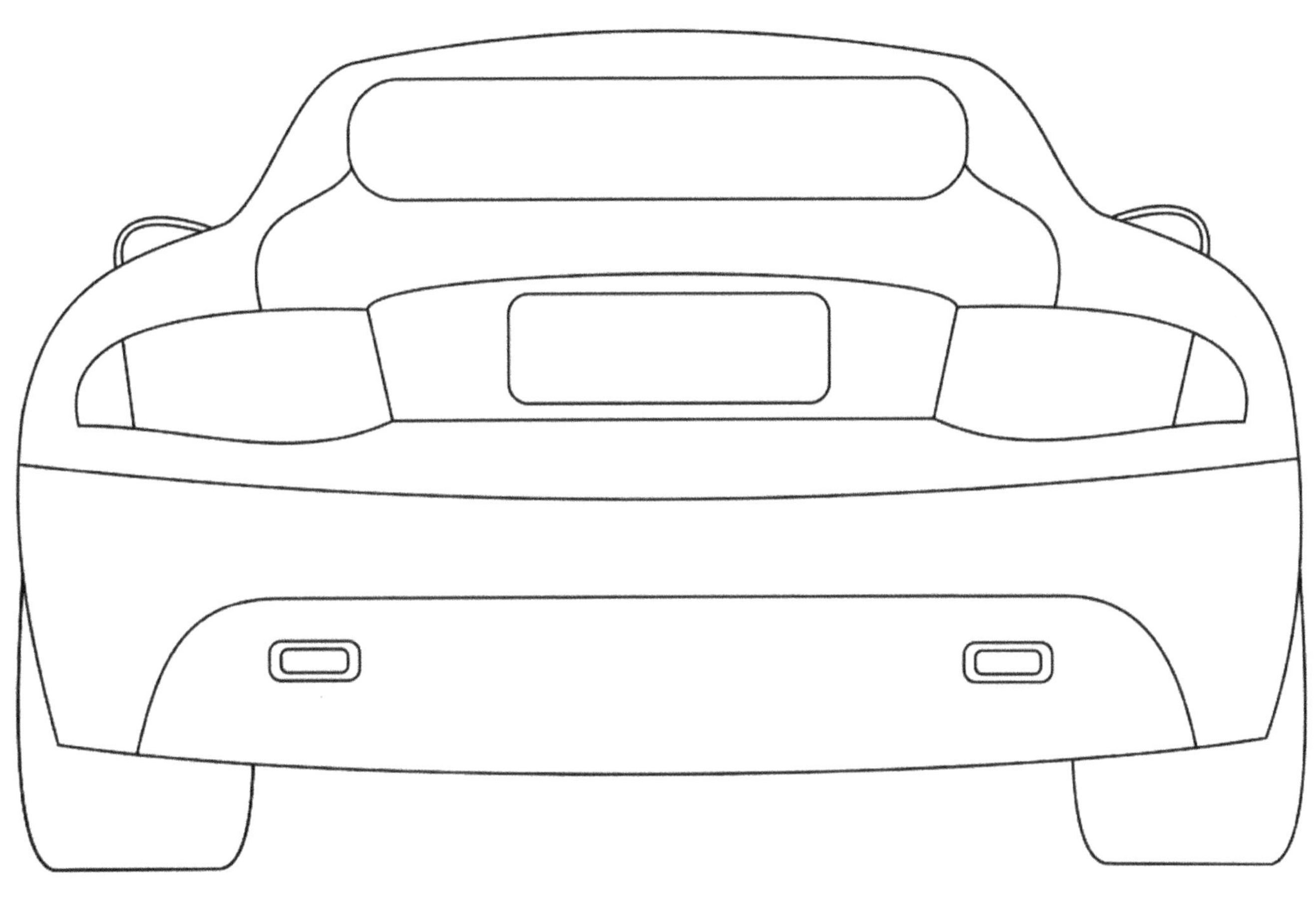

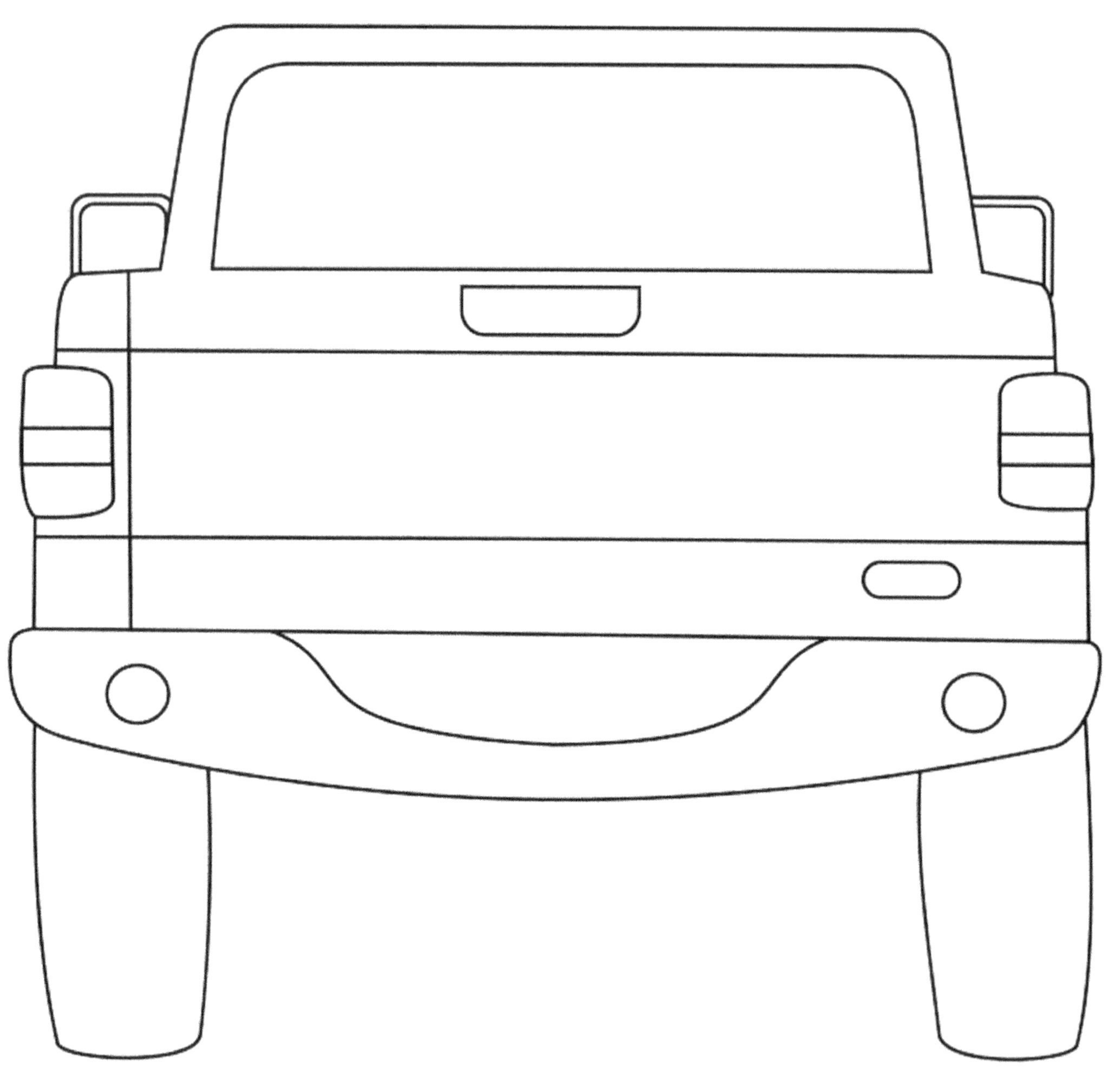

THANK YOU FOR YOUR PURCHASE!

We greatly appreciate your support. Without you, none of this would be possible. Please consider leaving us a review on Amazon.

Reviews greatly help us to be able to continue to produce books such as this one. Also, feel free to follow us on our social media channels or contact us directly at sketchpert.press@gmail.com

And be sure to join our exclusive Facebook Group for freebies, giveaways, and early preview copies!

@sketchperts

@sketchperts